First World War
and Army of Occupation
War Diary
France, Belgium and Germany

23 DIVISION
Divisional Troops
194 Machine Gun Company
12 December 1916 - 31 October 1917

WO95/2178/1

The Naval & Military Press Ltd
www.nmarchive.com
Published in association with The National Archives

Published by

The Naval & Military Press Ltd

Unit 10 Ridgewood Industrial Park,

Uckfield, East Sussex,

TN22 5QE England

Tel: +44 (0) 1825 749494

www.naval-military-press.com

www.nmarchive.com

This diary has been reprinted in facsimile from the original. Any imperfections are inevitably reproduced and the quality may fall short of modern type and cartographic standards.

© Crown Copyright
Images reproduced by permission of The National Archives, London, England, 2015.

Contents

Document type	Place/Title	Date From	Date To
Heading	WO95/2178/1 194th Machine Gun Coy 1916 Dec-1917 Oct		
Heading	23rd Division 194th Machine Gun Coy. Dec 1916 1917 Oct To Italy		
War Diary	Southampton	12/12/1916	12/12/1916
War Diary	Havre	13/12/1916	14/12/1916
War Diary	Belgium	16/12/1916	27/02/1917
War Diary	F. R.A.N.C.E.	28/02/1917	28/02/1917
Operation(al) Order(s)	194th Machine Gun Company Operation Order No. 1	19/02/1917	19/02/1917
Miscellaneous	Time Table Elevations and Compass Bearings		
Miscellaneous	194th Machine Gun Company Report On Operation Of 20th Feb 1917	20/02/1917	20/02/1917
War Diary	France	01/03/1917	05/04/1917
War Diary	Belgium	04/04/1917	05/04/1917
Heading	War Diary For March 1917 Of 19-M.G. Coy. Appendix I		
Miscellaneous	194 Machine Gun Company Operation Order No. 2	07/04/1917	07/04/1917
War Diary	Belgium	06/04/1917	02/05/1917
War Diary	France	03/05/1917	10/05/1917
War Diary	Belgium	11/05/1917	06/06/1917
Miscellaneous			
Miscellaneous	Operation Order No. 1	06/06/1917	06/06/1917
War Diary	Belgium	07/06/1917	15/06/1917
War Diary	France	16/06/1917	28/06/1917
War Diary	Belgium	29/06/1917	30/06/1917
Map	Trench Map		
War Diary	Belgium	01/07/1917	23/07/1917
War Diary	France	24/07/1917	31/07/1917
War Diary	Belgium	01/08/1917	05/08/1917
War Diary	France	06/08/1917	09/08/1917
War Diary	Belgium	28/08/1917	31/08/1917
War Diary	France	03/09/1917	20/09/1917
War Diary	Belgium	20/07/1917	02/10/1917
War Diary	France	03/10/1917	13/10/1917
War Diary	Belgium	14/10/1917	25/10/1917
War Diary	France	26/10/1917	31/10/1917

WO 95 2178/1

194th Machine Gun Coy

1916 Dec - 1917 Oct

23RD DIVISION

194TH MACHINE GUN COY.

DEC 1916-DEC 1918

1917 OCT

TO ITALY

23RD DIVISION

Army Form C. 2118.

WAR DIARY
or
INTELLIGENCE SUMMARY

(Erase heading not required.)

Instructions regarding War Diaries and Intelligence Summaries are contained in F. S. Regs., Part II. and the Staff Manual respectively. Title Pages will be prepared in manuscript.

194 Inf. Bde. S. Coy
Vol 1

Dec 16.
Dec 18

Place	Date	Hour	Summary of Events and Information	Remarks and references to Appendices
SOUTHAMPTON	12.12.16	5.0pm	Embarked.	
HAVRE.	13.12.16	1.0am	Disembarked. One G.S. Wagon and 2 Horses drawn, A.S.C. driver attached.	
		5.0pm	Arrived No.1. Rest Camp.	
	14.12.16	6.0pm	Departed No.1. Rest Camp.	
		6.0pm	Entrained Gare de Marchandaise.	
BELGIUM.	16.12.16	12.30am	Arrived Godewaersvelde.	
		12.m/d	Departed Godewaersvelde.	
		5.0pm	Arrived South Vlamertinghe.	
			Attached 23rd Division. B.E.7.	
	16.12.16			
	17.12.16.		Cooke. R. Pte. No 55111. Admitted to Hospital.	
			Williams. A. " " " 55181. " " "	
			Fell. E.T. L/Cpl. " 55131 Evacuated to No 2 C.C.S.	
			Tapping. W. Pte. " 55150. Admitted to D.R.S. Hospital.	
	18.12.16		Evans. H. Driver. " 313S4 " - D.R.S.	
	19.12.16		Inspected by Major Weiss. act/D. M.G.O.	
	19.12.16.		. NIL .	
	20.12.16.		No 46718.	
	21.12.16.		NIL.	
	22.12.16.		East. G. Pte. admitted to D.R.S.	

Army Form C. 2118.

WAR DIARY
or
INTELLIGENCE SUMMARY

(Erase heading not required.)

Place	Date	Hour	Summary of Events and Information	Remarks and references to Appendices
BELGIUM.	22.12/15		PRESTON. W. PTE. No 57109 admitted to D.R.S. MILLS. C.H. PTE. No 55142. discharged from D.R.S. EVANS. H. " " 31354. discharged from 71st F.A.	
	23.	9·30 am	DARBY. G. Cpl. No 53350. admitted to D.R.S. Company Inspected by Lt. Col. Martin 10th Coys Machine Gun Officer.	
	24.		COOK. R. Pte No 55111 discharged from Hospital.	
	25.		DARBY. G. Corporal. No 53350. discharged from D.R.S.	
	26.		EVANS. H. Pte. No 31354. admitted to 71st F.A. Four Officers and 60 other Ranks attached to 70th Machine Gun Company for Instruction in Trenches.	

Army Form C. 2118.

WAR DIARY
or
INTELLIGENCE SUMMARY
(Erase heading not required.)

Place	Date	Hour	Summary of Events and Information	Remarks and references to Appendices
BELGIUM.	27.		WILLIAMS. A. Pvt No 55181 Discharged from Hospital. ATKINSON. R. " " 34934. Admitted to D.R.S. DARBY. G. Corpal " 53350. Admitted to D.R.S.	
	28.		PARR. J. Pvt. No 58068. Admitted 71st F.A. BURGESS. L. " " 55134. " to D.R.S. MACDIARMID. J. " " 57892. " " D.R.S. STEPHENS. E. " " 55177. " " D.R.S. LOVE. R. Dr " 31073. " " D.R.S. & F.A. TAPPING. W. Pvt. " 55150. Discharged from 69 & F.A. PRESTON. W.H. Pvt. No 57109 " " 69 & F.A.	
	29.		ATKINSON. W. Pvt. No 31119. Admitted D.R.S. LETTS. E. L/Cpl. " 55169. " D.R.S. EAST. G.W. Pvt. " 46718. Discharged. D.R.S. DARBY. G. Corpal. " 53350. " D.R.S.	

Army Form C. 2118.

WAR DIARY
or
INTELLIGENCE SUMMARY

(Erase heading not required.)

Place	Date	Hour	Summary of Events and Information	Remarks and references to Appendices
BELGIUM.	29.		BURGESS. L. Pvt. No 55134. Discharged. D.R.S.	
			MacDIARMID. J. " " 57892. " D.R.S.	
			STEPHENS. E. " " 55177 " D.R.S.	
			LOVE. R. Dr. " 31073 " D.R.S.	
			Lieut. MUNRO. D.G. and 2/Lt BECKETT. N. with 38 other ranks and 6 guns. relieved 10 Info Cavalry Anti-Aircraft Section at ABEELE.	
			Lieut. J. R. DOVENER and 2/Lts G.B. MOIR and 2/Lt MURRAY B. rejoined from 70th Brigade. M.G. Coy.	
			THOMPSON. A. Pvt No 4330. of 10th NORTHUMBERLAND FUSILIERS. attached as a Second Cold Shoer.	
	30.		EAST. G.W. Pvt. No 46718. evacuated to M.G. Base. CAMIERS.	UNFIT. duty at FRONT.
			AUTHORITY. A/338/2/10	
			SMITH. C.H. Pvt. No. 42969 Admitted to D.R.S.	
			KENNEDY. W. Pvt. " 31380. " D.R.S.	
			LAW. J. L/Cpl. " 13509 " D.R.S.	
			ATKINSON. R. Pvt. No 34934. Evacuated to 3rd C.C.S.	

Army Form C. 2118.

WAR DIARY
or
INTELLIGENCE SUMMARY
(Erase heading not required.)

Place	Date	Hour	Summary of Events and Information	Remarks and references to Appendices
Belgium.	31.		Letts. E. L/Cpl. No. 55169. Discharged from D.R.S.	
			Atkinson. W. Pvte. No. 31119. " " D.R.S.	
			Smith. C.H. " 42969 " " D.R.S.	
			Law. J. Hop. " 31380 " " D.R.S.	
			Kennedy, W. Pte. No. 31386 Discharged to duty from D.R.S.	

Army Form C. 2118.

WAR DIARY
or
INTELLIGENCE SUMMARY

(Erase heading not required.)

194 M. G. Coy.

Place	Date	Hour	Summary of Events and Information	Remarks and references to Appendices
BELGIUM	4.1.17.		LAW. J. L/Cpl. No 13509. Driver. To duty from 70th F.A. PARR. J. Pvt. No 50068. " " " 70th F.A. Six men returned from Trenches.	G.C.
	5.1.17.		EDWARDS. F.T.J. Pvt No 50361. Wounded by Bomb dropped from Aeroplane. Flying over Vlamertinge.	J.S.C.
	6.1.17.		One man returned from the Trenches. EDWARDS F.T.J. Pvt No 50361. Evacuated to 17th C.C.S.	J.S.C.
	7.1.17.		ATKINSON. W. Driver No 31119. To duty from 69th F.A. SMITH. C.H. Driver No 42969 " " " 69th F.A.	J.S.C.
	8.1.17.		STEPHENS. E. Pvt No 55177 to D.R.S. ARUNDEL. G. " No 26663 " D.R.S.	G.C.

Army Form C. 2118.

WAR DIARY
or
INTELLIGENCE SUMMARY

(Erase heading not required.)

194 M.G. Coy

Place	Date	Hour	Summary of Events and Information	Remarks and references to Appendices
BELGIUM.	9.1.17.		SERRIDGE. G. Pte No 7558. To duty from 69th F.A. DOWNIE. A. Pte. No 34456 Evacuated 13th Stationary Hospital.	J.S.C.
	10.1.17.		PRESTON. W. H. Pte No 57109. admitted to 69th F.A.	J.S.C.
	11.1.17.		NIL.	J.S.C. 2/Lt Batchelor.
	12.1.17		One officer and 48 N.C.O.s men rejoined from trenches. DEWAR. W. Sergt. No 43949 admitted to 64th F.A.	J.S.C.
	13.1.17		Lieut DOVENER. 2/Lt MACK and 35 other Ranks proceeded to ABEELE. to take over Anti-Aircraft defences. LONG. G. Pte No 55118 admitted to 69th F.A. Lieut. MUNRO. 2/Lt. BECKETT. and 34 men rejoined from ABEELE.	J.S.C.

Army Form C. 2118.

WAR DIARY
or
INTELLIGENCE SUMMARY

(Erase heading not required.)

194 M. G. Coy

Place	Date	Hour	Summary of Events and Information	Remarks and references to Appendices
BELGIUM.	14/15		2/Lt BECKETT and 48 other ranks attached to 68th M.G. Coy for instruction in Trenches.	J.C.
	15/17		Weather very damp and cold.	J.C.
	16/17		Snow covered ground about ½ inch high. Major WEISS. D.M.G.O. Inspected the camp.	J.C.
	17/17		3 inches of snow fell during day.	J.C.
	18/17		Frost and very cold weather.	J.C.
	19/19		Freezing all day.	J.C.

Army Form C. 2118.

WAR DIARY
or
INTELLIGENCE SUMMARY

(Erase heading not required.)

194 M.G. Coy

Place	Date	Hour	Summary of Events and Information	Remarks and references to Appendices
Belgium	20/12/17		Freezing all day.	J.C.
	21/12/17		Freezing all day.	J.C.
	22/12/17		Lt Munro and 8 other Ranks proceeded to Trenches for Instruction. 2/Lt Beckett and 9 other Ranks rejoined from Trenches. 36337 Pte BAWDEN. H. Evacuated to No 2 Can: C.C.S.	J.C.
	23/12/17		Freezing all day.	J.C.
	24/12/17		Freezing all day.	J.C.

Army Form C. 2118.

WAR DIARY
or
INTELLIGENCE SUMMARY

(Erase heading not required.)

194 M. G. Coy

Place	Date	Hour	Summary of Events and Information	Remarks and references to Appendices
BELGIUM	25/17		SKIPPER. H. Pte. No 57116. WOUNDED in Trenches. Freezing all day. Two N.C.O.s to BASE.	J.C. A.G.6864 d/23/10/16
	26/17		Lieut. MUNRO. rejoined from trenches. Freezing all day.	J.C.
	27/17		Freezing all day.	J.C.
	28/17		Freezing all day. Twelve ranks relieved from trenches. 2/Lt BATCHELAR rejoined from Hospital	J.C.
	29/17		Freezing all day. Twelve ranks relieved from trenches.	J.C.

Army Form C. 2118.

WAR DIARY
or
INTELLIGENCE SUMMARY
(Erase heading not required.)

194 M. G. Coy.

Instructions regarding War Diaries and Intelligence Summaries are contained in F. S. Regs., Part II. and the Staff Manual respectively. Title Pages will be prepared in manuscript.

Place	Date	Hour	Summary of Events and Information	Remarks and references to Appendices
BELGIUM	30/1/17		One N.C.O. to Base. 12 Ranks relieved from Trenches.	A.C.6984. D 23/10/16 21/1/17
	31/1/17		Snow and hard frost after. No 57900. Pvt PRENTICE, A.O. Wounded by Shell Fire at VLAMERTINGE. JC	

2449 Wt. W14957/M90 750,000 1/16 J.B.C. & A. Forms/C.2118/12.

Army Form C. 2118.

Vol 3.
194 m. G. Coy

WAR DIARY
or
INTELLIGENCE SUMMARY

(Erase heading not required.)

Instructions regarding War Diaries and Intelligence Summaries are contained in F. S. Regs., Part II. and the Staff Manual respectively. Title Pages will be prepared in manuscript.

Place	Date	Hour	Summary of Events and Information	Remarks and references to Appendices
BELGIUM.	1.2.17		Freezing all day.	yc
	2.2.17.		Freezing all day.	yc
	3.2.17		Freezing all day.	yc
	4.2.17		Freezing all day.	yc
	5.2.17		Freezing all day.	yc.
	6.2.17		No 67995 Pvt. Watkins. G. No 45934 Pvt G. Gilchrist: S. To Company from Base.	
			Nos. 55091 Pvt. JOHNSON. A. J. and No 57115 Pvt. HART. A. Wounded in trenches.	yc.

2449 Wt. W14957/M90 750,000 1/16 J.B.C. & A. Forms/C.2118/12.

Army Form C. 2118.

WAR DIARY
or
INTELLIGENCE SUMMARY

(Erase heading not required.)

194. M. E. C.

Place	Date	Hour	Summary of Events and Information	Remarks and references to Appendices
Belgium.	6.2.17		No 55091 Pte JOHNSON. Evacuated to 2.C.C.S. No 57109 " PRESTON. W.H. Evacuated to 17.C.C.S.	J.C.
	7.2.17		Very Cold. Freezing Hard.	J.C.
	8.2.17		Very Cold. Hard Frost.	J.C.
	9.2.17		Cold & hard frost.	J.C.
	10.2.17		Cold and hard Frost. Nos 34480 Pte. HOY E.E. & No 17944 Pte WALTERS J.C. D. to Company from A.S.C. No 2 Depot. Section	J.C.
	11.2.17		Cold and sharp Frost.	J.C.

Army Form C. 2118.

WAR DIARY
or
INTELLIGENCE SUMMARY

(Erase heading not required.)

194 N. F. Coy

Place	Date	Hour	Summary of Events and Information	Remarks and references to Appendices
BELGIUM.	12.2.17.		Thaw set in.	JPC.
	13.2.17		Sunshine & No Frost. 2/Lt. C.R. LOWN proceeded to ENGLAND on 10 days Special Leave.	JPC.
	14.2.17	9.45p.m	About 30 High Explosive + Shrapnel Shells fell around Camp. No 58350 Pvt CANDY. W. Slightly wounded Right arm. Evacuated 2nd C.C.S.	JPC.
	15.2.17		Sharp Frost and Sunshine.	JPC.
	16.2.17		Very mild weather.	JC
	17.2.17		Very mild weather. 12 men Relieved from Trenches.	JPC.

Army Form C. 2118.

WAR DIARY
or
INTELLIGENCE SUMMARY
(Erase heading not required.)

Instructions regarding War Diaries and Intelligence Summaries are contained in F. S. Regs., Part II. and the Staff Manual respectively. Title Pages will be prepared in manuscript.

Place	Date	Hour	Summary of Events and Information	Remarks and references to Appendices
BELGIUM.	18/2/17		18.0. Ranks Relieved from Trenches. a/c N. BECKETT. Handed to Trenches. Nos. 68625 Pte T. R. S. R. 35781 Pte WALLIS. L. 67754 Pte McKAY. J. Joined Company from B.A.S.E.	pc.
	19/2/17		14.0. Ranks relieved from Trenches.	pc.
	20/2/17	8.55 6.40pm.	4 Guns assisted in Bombardment of Enemy Trenches.	Vide Appendix 1. pc.
	21/2/17		Very mild weather.	pc.

WAR DIARY
or
INTELLIGENCE SUMMARY

(Erase heading not required.)

Army Form C. 2118.

Place	Date	Hour	Summary of Events and Information	Remarks and references to Appendices
BELGIUM	22/2/17		No 37886 Pvt. CHRISTIE. J. Evacuated to 10.C.C.S. 70807 weather.	j.c.
	23/2/17		No. 58068. Pvt PARR. T. Evacuated to from N.C.C. " 58285 " ROTHERHAM H " to Base Hospital. MILD WEATHER.	j.c. j.c.
	24/2/17		Very mild weather.	
	25/2/17		Detachment from ABEELE rejoined Company. Lieut. C.R. LOWN. Rejoined from Leave to ENGLAND. 2/Lt N. BECKETT. and 40. O.R. rejoined from Trenches. No 27485 Pvt. WRIGHT. J.W. Evacuated to No 10.C.C.S.	j.c.

Army Form C. 2118.

WAR DIARY
or
INTELLIGENCE SUMMARY

(Erase heading not required.)

194 M.G. Coy.

Place	Date	Hour	Summary of Events and Information	Remarks and references to Appendices
BELGIUM.	26/2/17		Very mild WEATHER.	J.C.
	27/2/17	9.0 a.m.	Company moved to HERZEELE.	J.C.
FRANCE.	28/2/17	12 n/D.	Company moved to WULVERDINGHE.	J.C.

SECRET   Copy No. 2

194 Machine Gun Company
Operation Order No 1

Map Reference. ZILLEBEKE 1/10,000 Sheet 28 N.W.   19th Feb 1917

1. 140th Inf. Bde are carrying out a raid on an extensive scale on 20th Feb. To assist this 142nd Inf. Bde are having a dummy raid on the front of the left section of the Hill 60 Subsector.

2. 4 Machine Guns of 194th Coy M.G.C. will co-operate in the dummy raid and will search the rectangle formed by the following points I.29.d.2.0. I.29.d.8.0 — I.35.b.8.7. — I.35.a.3.7.

3. The 4 guns and 12 filled belts per gun will move to the specially selected positions in the trench running along the South bank of ZILLEBEKE LAKE between I.22.c.9.0. and I.22.d.3.0. during the night of 19th/20th Feb. They will be mounted and ready to fire at 4.40 pm on 20th Feb. They will be numbered 1 to 4 from right to left. No 1 & 2 under the command of 2nd Lieut B. MURRAY. No 3 & 4 under the command of Lieut D. G. MUNRO.

4. A time table and list of compass bearings and elevations is attached.

5. Zero hour will be 5.0 pm. 20th Feb.

6. Rapid fire will be maintained from Zero minus 5 to Zero plus 10 minutes. Intermittent fire from zero plus 10 to Zero plus 100 minutes. During the Intermittent firing intervals of 5 to 10 minutes between bursts of fire will occasionally be adopted — 2 guns ceasing fire at the same time.

7. At zero minus 5 minutes a mine will be exploded at I.29.c.70.15. At zero minus 2 minutes a mine will be exploded at I.29.c.7. Smoke grenades will be used and, if the wind is favourable, smoke can be also by the Infantry, also various coloured lights.

8. The guns will be taken out of action as soon after Zero plus 100 minutes as possible — they will not be moved until conditions are quite normal.

9. Acknowledge.

                                                                       H. V. Combs
                                                                           Captain
                                                            Commanding 194 Machine Gun Company

Issued at 5.0 pm
Copy No 1. File
        2. War Diary
        3. O.C. No 1 & 2 Guns
        4. O.C. No 3 & 4 Guns
        5. 23rd Division M.G.O.

194 Machine Gun Company

TIME TABLE, ELEVATIONS and COMPASS BEARINGS

	No 1 Gun		No 2 Gun		No 3 Gun		No 4 Gun	
	Magnetic Bearing	Quadrant Elevation	Magnetic Bearing	Quadrant Elevation	Magnetic Bearing	Quadrant Elevation	Magnetic Bearing	Quadrant Elevation
4.55 p.m. to 5.0 p.m	157½°	5° 18'	156½°	6°	157°	5° 30'	155½°	5°
5.0 p.m to 5.10 p.m	162½°	7° 10'	Traverse between 156½° and 160°	6°	162¼°	6° 30'	Traverse between 155½° and 161½°	5°
5.10 p.m to 6.40 p.m	Traverse between 156½° and 162½°	Search from 6° 40' to 7° 20'	Traverse between 156½° and 160°	Search from 5° to 7°	Traverse between 159¼° and 164¼°	Search from 5° 45' and 6° 40'	Traverse between 155½° and 161½°	4° 45' to 6°
6.40 p.m								

19/2/17

H. V. Combs.
Captain
Commanding 194 Machine Gun Company

194 Machine Gun Company

Report on Operations of 20th Feb 1917

The 4 guns came into action at 4.55 p.m this evening according to the programme and operation order. The programme was carried out without a hitch from start to finish and when the guns were dismounted, 12,500 rounds had been fired. N°1 gun had some shells within a few yards of it, N°s 2 & 3 had an easy time — nothing but splinters and a little shrapnel. N°4 was close to ZILLEBEKE and the "heavies" coming in there were near enough to be unpleasant. The guns were removed from the trenches when Hugg's Lodge pulled down at 8.15 p.m — we had no casualties.

H.V. Combs
Captain
O.C 194 M.G Coy

The following communication was dated 21/2/17 was received from the G.O.C. 47th Division addressed to 23rd Division — "Would you please express my thanks to the Artillery and Machine Gunners of your Division for the very great help given this Division during the recent raid. Their co-operation was of the highest importance to the success of the operation and was most effectively carried out."

Note: The raid was in the daylight and the enemy's trenches were occupied nearly 1½ hours. Over 100 prisoners were taken including 5 Machine Guns.

Army Form C. 2118.

WAR DIARY
or
INTELLIGENCE SUMMARY
(Erase heading not required.)

194 M.G. Coy.

Vol 4

Place	Date	Hour	Summary of Events and Information	Remarks and references to Appendices
FRANCE	1.3.17		Company. moved to Billets at OUEST. MONT.	J.C.
	2.3.17		Very mild weather.	J.C.
	3.3.17		Very mild weather.	J.C.
	4.3.17		No 55161 Pvt. YOUNG. P.J. died at 17. C.C.S	J.C.

Instructions regarding War Diaries and Intelligence Summaries are contained in F. S. Regs., Part II. and the Staff Manual respectively. Title Pages will be prepared in manuscript.

Army Form C. 2118.

WAR DIARY
or
INTELLIGENCE SUMMARY
(Erase heading not required.)

194 M.G. Coy.

Place	Date	Hour	Summary of Events and Information	Remarks and references to Appendices
FRANCE	5.3.17		No 36750 Pvt. McCANCE. T.J. Joined Company from M.G.C. Base.	
			" 68636 " SAVILLE. W.T. " " " " "	
			" 34456 " DOWNIE. G. " " " " "	
			" 68645 " STANNARD. 7. H.C. " " " " "	
			" 58068 " PARR. J. rejoined Company.	p.c.
	6.3.17		Snow and Sleet. very cold weather.	p.c.
	7.3.17		Very cold weather.	p.c.
	8.3.17		Snow. Cold winds.	
			No 55131. L/Cpl. FELL. E.T. Joined Company from M.G.C. Base.	p.c.
			" 66842. Pvt. SMITH. H. " " " " "	p.c.
	9.3.17		Cold, wind and snow.	p.c.

Army Form C. 2118.

WAR DIARY
or
INTELLIGENCE SUMMARY

(Erase heading not required.)

194 M. G. Coy.

Place	Date	Hour	Summary of Events and Information	Remarks and references to Appendices
FRANCE	10.3.17		Very mild weather.	JC
	11.3.17		Nil.	JC
	12.3.17		Very wet day.	JC
	13.3.17		Tactical Exercises under D.M.G.O.	JC
			82186. L/Cpl. COCK. C.	
			82021. Pvt. BAUMBER. R.S.	
			83088. " BAKER. E. } Joined Company from Base.	
			62962. " BUTLER. V.G.	
			81580. " BLAYNEY. T.	
			6562 " GOUGH. T.A.	JC

Army Form C. 2118.

WAR DIARY
or
INTELLIGENCE SUMMARY

(Erase heading not required.)

194th E. Coy

Place	Date	Hour	Summary of Events and Information	Remarks and references to Appendices
FRANCE	14.3.16		Very mild weather.	J.C.
	15.3.16		55113. Pvt. SLOWE. A.J. Evacuated to Base 28.2.17 Official Notice received today.	J.C.
	16.3.16		Very mild weather.	J.C.
	17.3.16		Spring weather. 12 Hours sunshine.	J.C.
	18.3.16		Spring weather. No 5452 BELL. R.B. L/Cpl. Evacuated 10th S.H.	J.C.

Army Form C. 2118.

WAR DIARY
or
INTELLIGENCE SUMMARY
(Erase heading not required.)

194 M.G. Coy.

Place	Date	Hour	Summary of Events and Information	Remarks and references to Appendices
FRANCE.	19 3/16		Company moved to Billets at MILLAIN.	p.c.
	20 3/16		Very cold weather.	p.c.
	21 3/16		Company moved to Billets at ESQUELBECQ.	p.c.
	22 3/16		Very cold weather. Snow.	p.c.
	23 3/16		Cold weather.	p.c.

Army Form C. 2118.

WAR DIARY
or
INTELLIGENCE SUMMARY
(Erase heading not required.)

194 M. G. Cy

Place	Date	Hour	Summary of Events and Information	Remarks and references to Appendices
FRANCE.	24/3/16		Very mild weather	J.C.
	25/3/16		Glorious Spring day. 62962. Pte. BUTLER. V. Evacuated to No.7. G.H. SUMMER Time started.	J.C.
	26/3/16		Cold Weather.	J.C.
	27/3/16		Cold Weather.	J.C.

Army Form C. 2118.

WAR DIARY
or
INTELLIGENCE SUMMARY
(Erase heading not required.)

194. M.G.C.

Instructions regarding War Diaries and Intelligence Summaries are contained in F. S. Regs., Part II. and the Staff Manual respectively. Title Pages will be prepared in manuscript.

Place	Date	Hour	Summary of Events and Information	Remarks and references to Appendices
FRANCE	28/3/17		Spring weather.	p.c.
	29/3/17		Wet day.	pc
	30/3/17		Very wet day.	pc.
	31/3/17		Very wet day.	pc.

2449 Wt. W14957/M90 750,000 1/16 J.B.C. & A. Forms/C.2118/12.

Army Form C. 2118.

WAR DIARY
or
INTELLIGENCE SUMMARY

(Erase heading not required.)

194 M.G. Coy.

Vol 5

Place	Date	Hour	Summary of Events and Information	Remarks and references to Appendices
FRANCE. 1.4.17			Very cold and wet day.	gc.
	2.4.17		Snow and very cold.	gc
	3.4.17		Snow, very cold.	gc
BELGIUM. 4.4.17			Company moved to Billets at WATOU.	gc.
	5.4.17		Company moved to OTTAWA CAMP near RENINGHELST. No 36750 Pvt McCANCE, T.J. ordered by A.D.M.S. to proceed to BASE.	gc.

WAR DIARY FOR MARCH
1917 OF 19A M.G.COY.

APPENDIX I

194 Machine Gun Company.

Operation Order No 2.   7th April 1917.

Map Reference ZILLEBEKE 1/10000 Sheet 28 N.W.

1. 47th Division are carrying out a large raid in daylight this evening. Their left Brigade is assisting by a dummy raid on HILL 60.
    Smoke and various coloured rockets will be used and a small mine exploded at HILL 60.
    There will also be a Dummy raid on ST ELOI CRATER

2. 4 Machine Guns of 194 M.G. Company will co-operate in the dummy raid, and will search the rectangle formed by the following points. I.29.d.60.00 – I.30.c.00.00 to I.35.d.60.60. – I.36.c.60.00.

3. 3 guns of No 3 Section and 1 from No 2 Section with 3500 rounds per gun will move to specially selected positions in trench on South bank of ZILLEBEKE LAKE about I.22.d.2.9. by 3.0 PM today. They will be mounted ready to fire at 7-40 PM. They will be numbered 1 to 4 from right to left. Nos 1 & 2 under the command of Lieut C.R. LOWN. Nos 3 & 4 under 2nd Lieut N. BECKETT under supervision of O.C No 3 Section.

4. A time-table for each gun and list of compass bearings and elevations is attached.

5. Zero hour will be 8-0 P.M.

6. Rapid fire will be maintained from Zero minus 5 minutes to Zero plus 10 minutes.
    Intermittent fire from Zero plus 10 minutes to Zero plus 65 minutes. During intermittent

firing intervals of from 5 to 10 minutes between bursts of fire will occasionally be adopted, 2 guns ceasing fire at the same time.

7. The 4 guns will be removed to their battle positions as soon after Zero plus 60 minutes as possible, but not before conditions are normal.

8. Acknowledge.

H. V. Cobb. Captain
Commanding 194 M.G. Cy.

Issued 2-0 P.M.
Copy No 1. File
      2 War Diary
      3 O.C No 3 Section

Army Form C. 2118.

WAR DIARY
or
INTELLIGENCE SUMMARY
(Erase heading not required.)

19 4 M. A. Coy

Place	Date	Hour	Summary of Events and Information	Remarks and references to Appendices
BELGIUM	6.4.17		No 36750 Pvt Mc.CANCE T.J. proceeded to Base. Company relieved 10 guns of 39th division and 2 guns of 47th division, in the Trenches.	p.c.
	7.4.17		Four Guns of the Company coperated with 47th division's Raid. See APPENDIX. No 1.	See No 1 APPENDIX. y.c
	8.4.17		No.55170 Pvt MILLBURN. J. Killed by Shell fire. Very cold weather.	p.c

WAR DIARY
INTELLIGENCE SUMMARY

Army Form C. 2118.

194 M.G. Coy

Place	Date	Hour	Summary of Events and Information	Remarks and references to Appendices
BELGIUM.	9/4/17	7.0am	Heavy bombardment of whole of Divisional Front the whole day until about 6.0pm then ceased for about 25 minutes.	
		6.25pm	Heavy Bombardment restarted	
		6.40pm	S.O.S sent up from Right Sector, Germans entered our trenches, but were immediately turned out, leaving several dead and wounded.	
		7.15pm	S.O.S sent up from LEFT Sector, Germans entered trenches, but not in force, being immediately killed, leaving several dead.	
			Our Guns opened fire on Barrage lines and fired our 10,000 rounds. ALL Ranks behaved splendidly, we had no Casualty (very slightly wounded.)	
			No.166511 L/Cpl DEWHURST. The Guns remained in action throughout in spite of a very heavy Barrage especially around OBSERVATORY Ridge and Rudkin House. Comms. Two were partially buried by shells and temporary put out of action. The Tunnel was blown in, in 7 places, also 3 of the Gun emplacements were demolished. Telephone Communication was maintained throughout between Company H.Q and the advanced Guns. This was mostly due to two of the Company Signallers who repaired wire totally during the bombardment.	Y/C
		6.15pm	Several Tear shells fell near Coy. H.Q. and filled it with gas. Vicinity of	Y/C
		8.15pm	which was bombarded throughout the day.	Y/C
	10/4/17		No. 62962 Pte BUTLER. V.G. W[ounded] for EVACUATION.	Y/C

Army Form C. 2118.

194 M.G. Coy.

WAR DIARY
or
INTELLIGENCE SUMMARY

(Erase heading not required.)

Instructions regarding War Diaries and Intelligence Summaries are contained in F.S. Regs., Part II and the Staff Manual respectively. Title Pages will be prepared in manuscript.

Place	Date	Hour	Summary of Events and Information	Remarks and references to Appendices
BELGIUM	11/4/17		Very cold weather and severe snowstorm. No 57118 Pte FEASEY. A. wounded by Shell Fire. No 4 Section relieved No 1 Section during night 10/11th.	J.C.
	12/4/17	5.30am	The Battery situated near Company H.Q. was heavily shelled, about 150 - 5.9 Shells being sent over by the Enemy.	
		8.0pm	Heavy Bombardment on LEFT of SALIENT.	J.C.
	13/4/17		Situation Normal. Very damp weather.	J.C.
	14/4/17		No 55147 Pte HATCHER. J. Killed by Shell Fire. No 55145 " CAWES. M.A. Wounded by Shell Fire and Evacuated. No 1 Section Attached to 60th Brigade.	J.C.

Army Form C. 2118.

194 M.G. Coy.

WAR DIARY
or
INTELLIGENCE SUMMARY

(Erase heading not required.)

Place	Date	Hour	Summary of Events and Information	Remarks and references to Appendices
BELGIUM	15 4/17		Very quiet day. Rain all day. Cold.	
	16 4/17		Very quiet day.	O.C.
	17 4/17		Rain and Hail. No 1 Section rejoined Company.	O.C.
	18 4/17		No 1 Section relieved No 2 Section in trenches. Heavy fall of snow in early hours of the morning.	O.C.

Army Form C. 2118.

WAR DIARY
or
INTELLIGENCE SUMMARY

(Erase heading not required.)

194 M.G. Coy.

Instructions regarding War Diaries and Intelligence Summaries are contained in F. S. Regs., Part II. and the Staff Manual respectively. Title Pages will be prepared in manuscript.

Place	Date	Hour	Summary of Events and Information	Remarks and references to Appendices
BELGIUM.	19.4/17.		No. 55164 Pte. J. TARRANT. 7 Evacuated 17.C.C.S. Very quiet day. No. 14330 PT. THOMPSON A 10th NORTHUMBERLAND FUSILIERS attacked cholera accidentally wounded at TRANSPORT LINES.	
	20.4/17		84135 PT EBLING J. 8 & 748 PT. FORSE F.A. & 83742 PT. FISHER F. joined from BASE DEPOT. 14330 PT. THOMSON A. Evacuated Canadian C.C.S. Two Guns of No 3 section under Command of Lieut. C. R Lomm fired 4,000 Rounds on Enemy Dumps & Communication lines, by Indirect Searching Fire. Good Results obtained for Enemy retaliated on our own communication lines.	J.C.
	21.4/17		No II SECTION relieved No III SECTION in Trenches	BM.
	22.4/17		Very quiet day	BM

Army Form C. 2118.

WAR DIARY
or
INTELLIGENCE SUMMARY

(Erase heading not required.)

194 M.G. COY.

Place	Date	Hour	Summary of Events and Information	Remarks and references to Appendices
BELGIUM	23/4/17		Heavy artillery activity on both sides the whole day.	
	24/4/17		No 45633 Pt. HOLT. J.H. killed by shell fire at VLAMERTINGHE No 9446 Pt. HOPPER. E. killed by shell fire ,, ,, Heavy artillery activity on both sides the whole day.	BM BM.
	25/4/17		Heavy artillery activity on both sides the whole day.	BM
	26/4/17		Heavy artillery activity on both sides the whole day.	BM

Army Form C. 2118.

WAR DIARY
or
INTELLIGENCE SUMMARY
(Erase heading not required.)

194 M.G. COY.

Place	Date	Hour	Summary of Events and Information	Remarks and references to Appendices
BELGIUM.	27/4/17		Heavy artillery activity on both sides the whole day.	B.M.
	28/4/17		Heavy artillery activity on both sides the whole day. No. 55158 L/CPL. STONE N. wounded by shell fire.	B.M.
	29/4/17		Very quiet day.	B.M.
	30/4/17		Very quiet day. During the Company's tour in the trenches very successful indirect overhead searching fire has been carried out on several occasions.	B.M.

Army Form C. 2118.

WAR DIARY
or
INTELLIGENCE SUMMARY
(Erase heading not required.)

Instructions regarding War Diaries and Intelligence Summaries are contained in F.S. Regs., Part II. and the Staff Manual respectively. Title Pages will be prepared in manuscript.

1940V M. G. C.

Vol 6

Place	Date	Hour	Summary of Events and Information	Remarks and references to Appendices
BELGIUM	1.5.17		Very quiet day.	
	2.5.17		Very quiet day. No. 86224 Pte. HARDY. A. } joined the Company from Base. " 86220 " HELKIN. C. } " 44712 " SAMUEL. A. }	g.c.
FRANCE	3.5.17		The Company was relieved by 57th M.G. Coy in the trenches on night of 2nd/3rd inst, and proceeded to Billets at STEENVOORDE.	g.c.
	4.5.17		Very quiet day.	g.c.
	5.5.17		Very warm day. G.O.C. 23rd Division inspected the Company.	g.c.
	6.5.17		Very warm day.	g.c.
	7.5.17		Very warm day. SHAW. F.W. L/Corp. No 55006. evacuated to 10.C.C.S.	g.c.

2449 Wt. W14957/M90 750,000 1/16 J.B.C. & A. Forms/C.2118/12.

Army Form C. 2118.

194 Coy M.G.C.

WAR DIARY
INTELLIGENCE SUMMARY
(Erase heading not required.)

Place	Date	Hour	Summary of Events and Information	Remarks and references to Appendices
FRANCE	8/5/17		Very warm day	
	9/5/17		The Company moved from STEENVOORDE and relieved 56 Coy M.G.C. in the trenches.	B.M
		10 PM	At 10 PM the GERMANS shelled trenches and communication trenches very heavily for about an hour, our artillery retaliated	
	10/5/17	3:45AM	GERMANS shelled our front & support lines very heavily in front of HILL 60. Our machine guns fired 13,000 rounds on barrage lines when S.O.S. went up. Germans entered trenches but were immediately evacuated.	B.M
			No 55168 CPL. WRIGHT C.F. } Gased in emplacement by fumes from " 55107 PTE. HAWKE C. } machine gun	
			VERY warm day	B.M

Army Form C. 2118.

194 Coy. M.G.C.

WAR DIARY
or
INTELLIGENCE SUMMARY
(Erase heading not required.)

Place	Date	Hour	Summary of Events and Information	Remarks and references to Appendices
BELGIUM	11/5/17	6.30AM	GERMANS shelled the BUND, S.W. Corner very heavily between 6.30 A.M. & 9.45 A.M. 293 shells fell between 8.30AM & 9.45 A.M. About 500 falling throughout the day. LIEUT B. MURRAY wounded. (at duty.) Very warm day No. 68062. MORTON.R. Co Ld Shoer. } joined the Company from home. " 9522 POWELL. W. Sadoller }	B.M. J.C.
	12/5/17		Very warm day.	
	13/5/17	3.30am	Germans heavily bombarded Brigade front and attempted a Raid but did not succeed. Nos. 55180 Pvt. HOLLY. M. } wounded & evacuated " 06220 " HELKIN.C. } The Tunnels around the Gun Positions were blown in in 7 places.	J.C.

Army Form C. 2118.

WAR DIARY
or
INTELLIGENCE SUMMARY

(Erase heading not required.)

194 M. G. Coy

Place	Date	Hour	Summary of Events and Information	Remarks and references to Appendices
BELGIUM	14/5/17		Coy H.Q at The Bund was shelled intermittently all day.	pc.
	15/5/17		Very warm day. Intermittent shelling on both sides during day	18m
	16/5/17		Very quiet day	18m
	17/5/17		Very quiet day	18m

Army Form C. 2118.

WAR DIARY
or
INTELLIGENCE SUMMARY

(Erase heading not required.)

194 Coy M.G.C.

Instructions regarding War Diaries and Intelligence Summaries are contained in F. S. Regs., Part II. and the Staff Manual respectively. Title Pages will be prepared in manuscript.

Place	Date	Hour	Summary of Events and Information	Remarks and references to Appendices
BELGIUM	18/5/17	9.30PM to 3.30AM	4 guns of this company fired 20,000 rounds on enemy communication lines, railways + dumps. Very quiet day.	BM
	19/5/17	9.30PM to 3.30AM	Very warm day. 4 guns of this company fired 30,000 rounds on enemy communication lines, railways + dumps. Heavy shelling during the day on both sides.	BM

2449 Wt. W14957/M90 750,000 1/16 J.B.C. & A. Forms/C.2118/12.

Army Form C. 2118.

194 Coy M.G.C.

WAR DIARY
or
INTELLIGENCE SUMMARY

(Erase heading not required.)

Place	Date	Hour	Summary of Events and Information	Remarks and references to Appendices
BELGIUM	20/5/17		Very warm day. Artillery activity on both sides during the day.	
		9.30PM to 3.30AM	Four guns of this company fired 31,000 rounds on enemy communication trenches, tramways & dumps during the night.	
			(20 men attached to company for duty) 3 from 10th WEST RIDING REGT 3 " 8th YORKS " 2 " 9th " " 2 " 11th WEST/YORKS " 10 " 11th N.F. "	BM
	21/5/17		Very warm day Artillery activity on both sides during day.	BM

Army Form C. 2118.

WAR DIARY
or
INTELLIGENCE SUMMARY.
(Erase heading not required.)

194 Coy. M. G. C.

Instructions regarding War Diaries and Intelligence Summaries are contained in F. S. Regs., Part II. and the Staff Manual respectively. Title pages will be prepared in manuscript.

Place	Date	Hour	Summary of Events and Information	Remarks and references to Appendices
BELGIUM	22/5/17	10 PM	Two guns fired 10,000 rounds on enemy communication trenches, tramways, and dumps. 55168 Cpl. WRIGHT C.F. suffering from M.G. fumes.	
		3. A.M.	Heavy artillery activity on both sides during day.	
			2nd LIEUT WHITFIELD joined from M.G. Base Depot.	BM
"	23/5/17		Very warm day. The Company was relieved in the trenches by 68th Coy M.G.C. on night of 23rd/24th & marched to WINNIPEG CAMP. 10 men from 8th YORK & LANCS attached for duty.	
"	24/5/17		Very warm day.	BM
"	25/5/17		Very warm day. 1 man attached for duty as loader from 1st LABOUR Bn 1st KINGS LIVERPOOLS.	BM
"	26/5/17		Very warm day. The following men to Base depot of 2nd ARMY No A/29/9. 59415 Pt NOLAN J. 58363 Pt DIGGORY F.W. 68645 Pt STANNARD F. 55105 A.SMITH A.C.W.F 83088 Pt BAKER E. 57123 Pt PRINCE E.	BM
"	27/5/17		Very warm day. CAPT. H.V. COMBS M.C. wounded slightly at duty.	BM
		10 PM	Enemy shelled WINNIPEG CAMP intermittently during night, the company bivouaced in a field	BM

Army Form C. 2118.

WAR DIARY
or
INTELLIGENCE SUMMARY.
(Erase heading not required.)

194 Coy. M.G.C.

Place	Date	Hour	Summary of Events and Information	Remarks and references to Appendices
BELGIUM	28/5/17		Very warm day. The company relieved 68th Coy M.G.C. in the trenches on night of 28/29th. Our communication lines were heavily shelled by enemy on night of 28th & the company had seven killed & wounded, also six mules & one horse killed.	
			37073 Pte LOVE R. } Killed by shell fire	
			31450 " WRIGHT C. }	
			34845 Sgt WILCOX T. }	
			55111 Pte COOK R. } Wounded by shell fire.	
			35349 " BULLOCK W. }	
			55092 " KITCHEN R.E. }	
			43403 " WEBB G. Wounded slightly at duty.	
				BM.

Army Form C. 2118.

WAR DIARY
or
INTELLIGENCE SUMMARY
(Erase heading not required.)

194 Coy M.G.C.

Place	Date	Hour	Summary of Events and Information	Remarks and references to Appendices
BELGIUM	29/5/17		Very warm day. Heavy artillery activity on both sides during day + night. One mule killed & one badly wounded.	Con.
"	30/5/17		Heavy artillery activity on both sides. 6000 Rounds were fired by our Guns on Enemy's Communication trenches, tramways and dumps between the hours of 10.0pm and 3.0am. No 55178 Pvt. LINHAM. G.H. wounded by shell fire.	J.O.C.
"	31/5/17		Heavy Shelling of Company Head Quarters. Our Guns fired 6000 Rounds on Enemy's tramways, dumps also searched his Communication trenches.	J.O.C.

Vol 7
194 Coy. M.G.C.

Army Form C. 2118.

WAR DIARY
or
INTELLIGENCE SUMMARY.
(Erase heading not required.)

Place	Date	Hour	Summary of Events and Information	Remarks and references to Appendices
BELGIUM	1/7	11:30AM to 1PM.	Enemy shelled Company Headquarters very heavily for an hour and a half.	
			Heavy artillery activity on both sides during day and night.	
			Six guns fired 6,000 rounds on enemy communications, tramways, and dumps.	
			LIEUT J.S. CRESSALL left to take over command of 107 Coy	
			M.G.C.	
			90139 Pte GILCHRIST T. ⎫	
			89920 Pte ROWLAND G.A. ⎬ Joined from M.G. Base Depot.	
			90339 Pte BOORER G. ⎪	
			90341 Pte DIGBY C. ⎭	
				RM.

Army Form C. 2118.

WAR DIARY
or
INTELLIGENCE SUMMARY.

19th Coy. M.G.C.

(Erase heading not required.)

Instructions regarding War Diaries and Intelligence Summaries are contained in F. S. Regs., Part II. and the Staff Manual respectively. Title pages will be prepared in manuscript.

Place	Date	Hour	Summary of Events and Information	Remarks and references to Appendices
BELGIUM	2/6/17		Very warm day	
			Heavy artillery activity on both sides during day & night	
		10 PM	Machine Gun fired 10,000 rounds on enemy communication trenches, tramways + dumps	
		3 AM	Heavy artillery activity on both sides during day & night	
"	3/6/17		Very warm day.	
		3.15 PM	Five guns fired 5,000 rounds on barrage lines during DIVISIONAL demonstration from 3.15 PM to 3-30 PM. Enemy retaliated heavily on trenches	
		3.30		
		10 PM	Seven guns fired 10,000 rounds on enemy communication trenches, tramways + dumps	
		3 AM		
		10.45 PM	Enemy shelled Company Headquarters with gas and tear shells from 10.45 PM to 4 AM.	
		4 AM	44712 PT. SAMUEL A. accidentally wounded. evacuated 4/6/17 13M	

Army Form C. 2118.

WAR DIARY
or
INTELLIGENCE SUMMARY.
(Erase heading not required.)

194 Coy M.G.C.

Place	Date	Hour	Summary of Events and Information	Remarks and references to Appendices
BELGIUM	4/7		Very warm day.	
			Heavy artillery activity during day & night.	
			One section 70th Coy M.G.C. relieved Nos 2 & 3 Sections in OBSERVATORY	
			RIDGE SECTOR on night of 2/5th. No 3 Section proceeded to VALLEY COTTAGES	
			& No 2 Section to ZILLEBEKE.	
		10 PM	Enemy shelled Coy Headquarters with tear & gas	
		12.45AM	shells from 10 PM to 12.45 A.M.	
			2nd LIEUT R.A. DRAPER.	
			89903 Pt. BAULEY A.E.	Joined from M.G.C. Base Depot.
			89509 " HART J.V.	
			89223 " HOWES P.F.	
			87061 " PITTUCK A.E.	
			89518 " STICKLES H.J.	
			89899 " TOWNSEND E.	
				BM

Army Form C. 2118.

194 Coy M.G.C.

WAR DIARY
~~INTELLIGENCE SUMMARY.~~
(Erase heading not required.)

Place	Date	Hour	Summary of Events and Information	Remarks and references to Appendices
BELGIUM	5/7/17		Heavy artillery activity on both sides. Company Headquarters shelled with tear & gas shells. Coy. Headqrs moved from BUND to ZILLEBEKE on night of 5/6 ult. Four guns fired 10,000 rounds on enemy tramways + dumps. 18M	
	6/7/17		Heavy artillery activity on both sides. Four guns fired 18000 rounds on enemy tramways + dumps. 55090 Pt HEDLEY W. wounded & evacuated 6/8/17. ~~579~~ Pt GILCHRIST 8M. 98081 Pt HOPLEY E. 98060 " EDWARDS T. 90135 " LARGE W. 90067 " LEE A. 57277 " FRANKCOM G. 89914 " SIRQVIRN W. } Joined from M.G. Base Depot. The Company moved into battle position on night of 6/7 ult. 8M	

Programme for 'K' and 'L' Batteries

UNIT	TIME	TARGET	RATE OF FIRE	REMARKS
19th Machine Gun Company	Zero hour to Z plus 40 Minutes	Dotted RED line between B and C	1 Belt per gun per 4 Minutes	
	Z plus 45 minutes to Z plus 1 hour 25 minutes	Dotted BLUE line between B and C	1 Belt per gun per 4 Minutes	
'L' Battery only	Z plus 1 hour 30 Minutes to Z plus 2 hours 30 Minutes	Dotted BLUE line in front of 'L' Battery	1 Belt per gun per 8 Minutes	Fire to be maintained on the flash while Battery is on moving forward
'K' Battery only	Z plus 2 hours 30 Mins to Z plus 3 hours 30 Mins	Dotted BLACK line in front of 'L' Battery	1 Belt per gun per 8 Minutes	-- ditto --
Both Batteries	Z plus 3 hours 40 Mins to Z plus 5 hours 5 Mins	Dotted BLACK line between B & C	1 Belt per gun per 4 Minute	

Note :— 1. At Zero plus 1 hour 30 Minute 'K' Battery will move forward to 'K' 2 position and be in the new position by Z plus 2 hours 30 Minute. At Z plus 2 hours 30 Minute 'L' Battery will move forward to L 2 position and be in the new position by Z plus 3 hours 30 Minute.
Not more than 2 guns to move at the same time
2. When the move is completed all Batteries will lay on normal barrage target and keep up a slow fire of 1 Belt per gun per 8 minute by 2 gun per battery
3. At Z plus 3 hours 5 Minute Lay on Dotted Yellow line also. Fire to be maintained by 2 gun per battery at the rate of 1 Belt per gun per 1 minute, with clock arm long range ranging up to 3000 yards will be maintained at intervals of about 20 minute throughout the night by 4 guns in each battery. In an S.O.S. all guns will fire on their barrage lines.

Secret   Copy No 4

Operation Order No 1 by Captain H.V. COMBS. M.C.
Commanding 194 Machine Gun Company 6.6.17

MAP REFERENCE. ZILLEBEKE 5A and WYTCHAETE.

The Second Army will attack the MESSINES-
WYTCHAETE Ridge.

1. The attack on the left flank by the 23rd
DIVISION will be supported by a Machine
Gun Barrage.
2. 194 M.G. Coy will form the left Group
of this Barrage.
3. The Group is divided into two Batteries
lettered "K" and "L", each composed of eight
guns. "K" Battery will be on the right under
the command of LIEUT B. MURRAY and "L"
Battery on the left under the command of
LIEUT D.G. MUNRO. Nos 1 and 4 Sections
will form "L" Battery. Nos 2 and 3 Sections
will form "K" Battery.
4. Battery positions, belt filling depots,
advanced store and repair shop, and
Group H.Q. are shewn on the attached map.
5. Table giving times of firing, targets and
moves to forward positions is attached
6. On Y/Z night "K" and "L" Batteries will

move into their rear battle positions. Batteries to be in position and all guns laid on their primary barrage lines by zero - 3 hours.

7 Battery Commanders will be prepared to direct fire at a moments notice on any point beyond the red line and to left or right of their front.

8 25 per cent of all ranks will be sent to the Transport lines on "X" day; the remaining spare men and carriers will be disposed as follows:- half will be in cellars at VALLEY COTTAGES under 2nd LIEUT N. BECKETT who will be responsible for sending out carriers to help both Batteries to get their belt boxes, water etc forward. He will personally inspect the vacated positions and collect and send forward anything left behind. The remainder in cellars at ZILLEBEKE under C.S.M. An equal proportion from each Battery will be at both places.

9 One R.A.M.C Private will be attached to each Battery from X/Y night. He must on no account be used as a Stretcher Bearer; spare men, if available, must be used for this.

10 Large openings must be cut on Y/Z night in all hedges which interfere with the line of fire in any direction.

11 Z day, zero hour and orders for

3.

synchronisation of watches will be issued later.

12. Battery Commanders will report to Group Headquarters at DORMY HOUSE at Zero – 2 hours 30 minutes that their Batteries are ready for the operations in every respect.

13. Batteries will report completion of their move to the advanced positions.

14. Casualties should be reported as soon as possible to enable the Group Commander to replace them from the advanced depot of spare men.

       J. R. Dovener Lieut
                for Captain
  Commanding 194 Machine Gun Company

10·0 am

No	Copy	
1	"	File
2	"	O.C K Battery
3	"	O.C L Battery
4	"	Base

Army Form C. 2118.

WAR DIARY
or
INTELLIGENCE SUMMARY.
(Erase heading not required.)

194 Coy M.G.C.

Place	Date	Hour	Summary of Events and Information	Remarks and references to Appendices
BELGIUM	7/6/17	3.10 AM	The Company came into action at 3.10 AM see appendix attached.	
			72473 PT HOWES R. ⎱ evacuated for duty from 69th F.A.	
			34471 " STEVENS H. ⎰	
			55173 L/CPL LUNNON W. Wounded + evacuated	
			55769 " LETTS E. shell shock + evacuated	
			45934 PT GILCHRIST S. Wounded remained at duty.	
				SM.
	8/6/17		67266 PT BECK N. shell shock at duty.	
			24279 PT BUTTERY H.E. ⎫	
			39210 " BOWERS W.I. ⎬ from A.H.T.D. 8/6/17	
			16410 " SEWELL G.F. ⎪	
			21380 " RODGERS J ⎭	
			Advanced gun positions shelled during day also VALLEY COTTAGES.	
			Kt BATTERY ES fired 30,000 rounds on dotted yellow line	
				SM

Army Form C. 2118.

WAR DIARY
or
INTELLIGENCE SUMMARY
(Erase heading not required.)

194 Coy M.G.C.

Place	Date	Hour	Summary of Events and Information	Remarks and references to Appendices
BELGIUM	9/7		Enemy shelled forward emplacements & VALLEY COTTAGES during day & mg.Kt. ZILLEBEKE heavily shelled. Our guns fired 16,000 rounds on enemy communication trenches.	18M.
	10/7		Enemy shelled forward positions & VALLEY COTTAGES. Our guns fired 10,000 rounds on enemy communication trenches. 12443 PT PUSEY G. wounded & evacuated 26663 " ARUNDEL G. shell shock evacuated 67995 " WATKINS G. wounded & evacuated 55175 " HOLDER P. wounded remained at duty	18M

Army Form C. 2118.

WAR DIARY
or
INTELLIGENCE SUMMARY

(Erase heading not required.)

194 Coy M.G.C.

Place	Date	Hour	Summary of Events and Information	Remarks and references to Appendices
BELGIUM	11/6/17		ZILLEBEKE very heavily shelled during day, forward position & VALLEY COTTAGES shelled intensively. LIEUT C.R. LOWN wounded & evacuated. 90339 PT BOORER G. wounded & evacuated. 11079 SGT SHERWOOD A. joined from A.H.T.D. Four guns fired 10,000 rounds on enemy communication trenches. 6M	
	12/6/17		Artillery activity on both sides during day & night. Very warm day. 6M	
	13/6/17		ZILLEBEKE very heavily shelled the whole day. Heavy artillery activity on both sides during day. 1M	
	14/6/17		ZILLEBEKE very heavily shelled the whole day with all calibre shells. Heavy artillery activity on both sides during day. Very warm day. 8M	

Army Form C. 2118.

WAR DIARY
or
INTELLIGENCE SUMMARY.
(Erase heading not required.)

194 Coy M.G.C.

Place	Date	Hour	Summary of Events and Information	Remarks and references to Appendices
BELGIUM	15/6/17		The Company moved out of the line on the morning of 15th and proceeded to Billets at BERTHEN. Very warm day.	
FRANCE	16/6/17		All men attached from infantry returned to their units. Very warm day.	BM
	17/6/17		2 R.A.M.C. attached returned to their units. Very warm day.	BM
	18/6/17		2nd LIEUT. H.R.P. PATTERSON joined from M.G.C. Base Depot. The Company were inspected by the G.O.C. 83rd Division. Very warm day.	BM

WAR DIARY
or
INTELLIGENCE SUMMARY
(Erase heading not required.)

Army Form C. 2118.

194 M.G.C.

Place	Date	Hour	Summary of Events and Information	Remarks and references to Appendices
			S.S.093 Cpl Tubb.E.G. S.S.17H L/Cpl Ledwith.S.	
			S.S.130 Pte Storrar 34416 Pte Downie.F. ⎫ Proceeded on a course	
			84748 " Forse.F.A. S.S.072 " Oaten.T. ⎬ of 1st Aid at the	
			S.S.305 " Neal.H.A. S.S.175 " Holder.P. ⎭ 69th Field Ambulance.	
			S.7110 " Harris.E. S.7111 " Tennant.J.A.	DJM
	19/7		Thunder & rain throughout the day & night.	
	20/6/17		9432 Pte Murray J. proceeded on course of Chiropody.	DJM
			Warm some rain	
	21/6/17		Cool some rain	DJM
	22/6/17		S.S.179 Pte Mayne proceeded on a course of cookery	DJM
			Showers throughout the day	
	23/6/17		S.S.124 Pte Goodchild C.G. rejoined from hospital. DJM	
			Mild some rain	DJM

Army Form C. 2118.

WAR DIARY
or
INTELLIGENCE SUMMARY.
(Erase heading not required.)

194 M.G.C.

Place	Date	Hour	Summary of Events and Information	Remarks and references to Appendices
France	24/6		90135 Pte Large W rejoined from hospital.	
			43949 Sgt Dennard W	
			37437 " Richardson W.H.	
			45.5714 " Pearson C.	
			28636 Cpl Edmondson S. ⎫ Were awarded the MILITARY MEDAL	
			16651 L/Cpl Dewhurst F.G. ⎬ dated 7-6-17	
			5.5.115 " Hart T.A. ⎪	
			5.5.13.3 Pte Green W.J. ⎪	
			34456 " Downie J. ⎭	R.B.M.
	25/6		89899 TOWNSEND ⎫	
			90135 LARGE W ⎬ were transferred to 69 M.G.C.	
			5.7277 FRANKCOM C. ⎪	
			89914 SIEQUIN W. ⎭	R.B.M.

Army Form C. 2118.

WAR DIARY
or
INTELLIGENCE SUMMARY.
(Erase heading not required.)

194 M.G.C.

Place	Date	Hour	Summary of Events and Information	Remarks and references to Appendices
France	26/6/17		Fine day. 8920 Pte ROWLAND. F. evacuated	J.B.Moir Lt.
"	27/6/17		Fine day.	J.B.M.
"	28/6/17		No 3 Section proceeded up the line and took over from 1 section of 191. M.G. Coy. Remainder of Coy. proceeded to MURRUMBIDGEE CAMP. Heavy thunderstorm during evening.	J.B.M.
Belgium	29/6/17		Company moved to MIC MAC CAMP. 55083 Pte MUGLESTON W. was admitted to hospital.	J.B.M.
"	30/6/17		Company moved to another portion of MIC MAC CAMP. Heavy rain throughout day.	J.B.M.

HILLEBERE
SHEETS 27NW & NE 9 (parts of)
EDITION 1.A

K + L BATTERIES

Army Form C. 2118.

WAR DIARY
or
INTELLIGENCE SUMMARY
(Erase heading not required.)

161 & 194 M.G. Coy

Place	Date	Hour	Summary of Events and Information	Remarks and references to Appendices
Belgium	1/7/17		89920 Pte ROWLAND.G. evacuated dated 27-6-17	O.9.M.
	2/7/17	5.5.15.0 P.M.	TAPPING.W. evacuated dated 27-6-17.	O.9.M.
	3/7/17		No II Sect relieved No III Sect in the line on this night 9/4/4.	O.9.M.
	4/7/17		2 guns teams of No III Sect went into the line	O.9.M.
	5/7/17		5.5.144 Cpl WRIGHT. C.F. was killed. 90341 Pte DIGBY.C.W. was wounded. 5.5.1001 Pte STONIER evacuated	O.9.M.
	6/7/17		2nd Lieut J. WHITFIELD } evacuated 5.3.144 Pte PENN H.W. } dated 3-7-17.	Jeo

Army Form C. 2118.

WAR DIARY
or
INTELLIGENCE SUMMARY
(Erase heading not required.)

Instructions regarding War Diaries and Intelligence Summaries are contained in F. S. Regs., Part II. and the Staff Manual respectively. Title Pages will be prepared in manuscript.

Place	Date	Hour	Summary of Events and Information	Remarks and references to Appendices
Belgium	7/7/17		Fine day. Situation normal. Working parties and transport unable to reach line owing to heavy shelling	J.E.D.
	8/7/17		Wet day. Transport again unable to reach line owing to shelling and congestion of traffic	J.E.D.
	9/7/17		5/5086 Pte SHAW F.W. rejoined from evacuation	
			45934 L/Cpl GILCHRIST S. } Killed	
			5/5166 Pte PARKER C. }	
			5/5082 Pte BOULTON A.J. Wounded	
			62962 " BUTLER V.G. chewing 8.7.17	J.E.D.
10/7/17			55131 2/Cpl FELL E.T. shell shock at duty	
			55084 Cpl TURNER J.F. } Killed	
			55129 Pte WILSON T. }	
			55099 " WONNACOTT W.A. }	
			62962 Pte BUTLER V.G. Returned, having become attached to another unit	J.E.D.
11/7/17			LIEUT N. SMART Joined from Base Depot 16 (otto Rocks) Infantry, 20th drid for duty in both filling during the offensive	J.E.D.

WAR DIARY
or
INTELLIGENCE SUMMARY

Army Form C. 2118.

Place	Date	Hour	Summary of Events and Information	Remarks and references to Appendices
Belgium	12/7/17		2/LIEUT G. H. TYNDALL joined from Base Depot	JRD
	13/7/17		34295 Cpl Tisdale R.W. Wounded	
			No 2 & 4 Sections came out of the trenches & rejoined the Company HQ at MICMAC CAMP	JRD
	14/7/17		16 O.R.s (Infantry) joined for duty for shell filling	JRD
			during the offensive	
	15/7/17		50158 L/Cpl STONE N	JRD
			81580 Pte BLAYNEY T.	
			90335 " LOVE C.E.	joined from M.G. Base Depot
			90125 " MALLIN J.	
			90493 " TITSHALL W.E.	
	16/7/17		Very hot day	JRD
	17/7/17		Wet day	JRD
	18/7/17		Wet day	JRD

WAR DIARY
or
INTELLIGENCE SUMMARY

(Erase heading not required.)

Army Form C. 2118.

Place	Date	Hour	Summary of Events and Information	Remarks and references to Appendices
Belgium	19/7/17		Shelled out of camp at 2.20 a.m. Returned to camp at 3.20 a.m.	DGM
	20/7/17		Hot day	DGM
	21/7/17		Hot day	DGM
	22/7/17		5-5-136 Pte Wyatt W.H. rejoined from evacuation. 3-5188 Pte Williams T.G. evacuated	DGM
	23/7/17		Hot day. 3326g Pte Hart wounded & evacuated. Company move to BERTHEN area	DGM
			Very hot day. LIEUT N. BECKETT to ENGLAND on duty. & H.Q. Escort	DGM
France	24/7/17		3-9132 Cpl THOMAS H. 6708 " Stedman R. 44317 " ABBOTT F. } Joined from M.G. Base Depot 24-7-17	DGM
	25/7/17		Very hot day	DGM
			Wet day	DGM
	26/7/17		Hot day. 37107 Pte RUSSELL H. evacuated 24-7-17. Very hot day	DGM

Army Form C. 2118.

194 M.G. Coy

WAR DIARY
or
INTELLIGENCE SUMMARY
(Erase heading not required.)

Place	Date	Hour	Summary of Events and Information	Remarks and references to Appendices
France	27/7/17		Very hot day	JHD
	28/7/17		Very hot day	JHD
	29/7/17		2/Lt. P.H. HOLGATE Joined from M.G. Base	JHD
		57.30	Pte STONIER W. Rejoined from Evacuation	
	30/7/17		The Company moved into the line, being attached to 41st Division.	
			2/Lt H.R. PATTERSON — Wounded	
		68636	Pte SAVILLE W. "	
		55174	L/Cpl LEDWITH S. "	
		90007	Pte LEE A. Died of wounds	JHD
	31/7/17		The 41st Division carried out an attack and the Company supported this with barrage fire. Ammunition expended 74,000 rounds against an enemy counter attack and harassing fire.	JHD

Army Form C. 2118.

WAR DIARY
or
INTELLIGENCE SUMMARY
(Erase heading not required.)

194 Machine Gun Coy

Place	Date	Hour	Summary of Events and Information	Remarks and references to Appendices
Belgium	1/8/17		Very wet day. 11139 Sgt EMMOTT F. gassed. Company fired on enemy counter attack, and carried out harassing fire during the night.	
	2/8/17		37045 Pte ANSELL E. joined from A.H.T.D. Weather still very wet. 55087 Pte OATEN T.E. } wounded 87067 PITTUCK A.E. } Company fired 40,000 rounds on barrage lines.	J.R.O. J.R.O. J.R.O.
	3/8/17		Weather still very wet. Fairly quiet day	
	4/8/17		Still wet. Fairly quiet.	
	5/8/17		The enemy attacked on HIR Div front in the early morning but was soon driven back. 56 357 Pte DAY G. Killed. The company was relieved by 23rd M.G. Company and on relief	J.R.O.
France	6/8/17		returned to BERTHEN The Company moved from BERTHEN to ARQUES	J.R.O.
	7/8/17		The Company moved from ARQUES to LE BUISSON	J.R.O. J.R.O.

WAR DIARY
or
INTELLIGENCE SUMMARY

Army Form C. 2118.

(Erase heading not required.)

Place	Date	Hour	Summary of Events and Information	Remarks and references to Appendices
France	8/8/17		Lt J. Russell-Jones S-336 Pte Ash P.R. 103288 " Henley O.J. 102425 " Hodson A. 8)321 " Harper C. 103305 " Humphrey A.H. } Joined from M.G. Base	Geo
	9/8/17		Company moved to Eperlecques Area 103892 Pte Benton H. 103889 " Black H.H. 104154 " Burton W. 104131 " Everson R. 104142 " Lingwood H. 104937 " McArthur J. 103895 " Page S.A. 104152 " Pike L. 90679 " Wooliams J.F. 270974 " Wragg J.H.	Geo

Army Form C. 2118.

WAR DIARY
or
INTELLIGENCE SUMMARY

(Erase heading not required.)

Instructions regarding War Diaries and Intelligence Summaries are contained in F. S. Regs., Part II. and the Staff Manual respectively. Title Pages will be prepared in manuscript.

Place	Date	Hour	Summary of Events and Information	Remarks and references to Appendices
France	10/8/17		65135 Pte POOLE A.	
			29992 " McKEON J.	
			57277 " FRANKCOM G.	
			145-79 " GILLAM R.	
			60342 " OLDHAM H.	
			97547 " HOPPER B.H. } Transferred from	
			97651 " PUGH T. } 69 M.G. Company	
			87416 " PASTEAU L.	
			72723 " PETCH C.	
			98037 " SPRATLING R.	
			68423 " SMITH F.R.	
			97625 " SCRIMGEOUR J.	
			97877 " STEEL J.	
			97696 " TATMAN G.W.	
			90860 " TEMPLIR F.A.	
	11/8/17		83742 " FISHER F. } Evacuated 41st C.C.S.	7600
	12/8/17		5-5435 " NEILSON L. } 8.8.17	7600
			Weather showery	7600

WAR DIARY
INTELLIGENCE SUMMARY
(Erase heading not required.)

Army Form C. 2118.

Place	Date	Hour	Summary of Events and Information	Remarks and references to Appendices
France	13/8/17		Fine day	JRO
	14/8/17		Fine day	JRO
	15/8/17		Fine day	JRO
	16/8/17		95791 Sgt HISLOP D. transferred to 70th M.G. Company on promotion.	
			57277 Pte FRANKCOM G. }	
			72723 " PETCH C. } To Base Depot	
			68423 " SMITH F.R. }	
			97877 " STEEL J }	
			83742 " FISHER F. Rejoined from evacuation	JRO
	17/8/17		Fine day	JRO
	18/8/17		Fine day	JRO
	19/8/17		The company marched to ENEMY Field firing range and bivouaced for the night	JRO

Army Form C. 2118.

WAR DIARY
or
INTELLIGENCE SUMMARY
(Erase heading not required.)

Instructions regarding War Diaries and Intelligence Summaries are contained in F.S. Regs., Part II. and the Staff Manual respectively. Title Pages will be prepared in manuscript.

Place	Date	Hour	Summary of Events and Information	Remarks and references to Appendices
France	20/9/17		The Company carried out Field firing practice and then returned to Billets	J.R.O.
	21/9/17		Fine day	J.R.O.
	22/9/17		Fine day	J.R.O.
	23/9/17		Fine day	J.R.O.
	24/9/17		The Company left WESTROVE and proceeded by train to the WIPPENHOEK AREA. LIEUT J.B. MOIR proceeded to VOLKERINCKHOVE for Course of Instruction. 31742 C.2. db. S. DE ROSE T transferred to 109 M.G. Coy on promotion.	J.R.O.
	25/9/17			J.R.O.
	26/9/17		The Company left the WIPPENHOEK AREA and proceeded by motor lorry to the DICKEBUSCH AREA. 13-197 C.2. db. S IBBOTSON W. joined from 59 M.G. Coy	J.R.O.
	27/9/17		Two sections proceeded to the line. Very wet day.	J.R.O.

Army Form C. 2118.

WAR DIARY
or
INTELLIGENCE SUMMARY
(Erase heading not required.)

Place	Date	Hour	Summary of Events and Information	Remarks and references to Appendices
Belgium	28/8/17		67200 Pte BIRCHALL D. rejoined from evacuation	
	29/8/17		104142 " LINGWOOD H. Wounded	FRO
			5-5-17) " STEPHENS E. "	FRO
	30/8/17		34295 Cpl TINDALE R. W rejoined from M. G. Base	FRO
			LIEUT J. RUSSELL-JONES Wounded.	
	31/8/17		5-5-08) Cpl ADAMS H.O. to CAMIERS for M.G. Course	FRO
			Two sections came out of the line	

WAR DIARY
INTELLIGENCE SUMMARY

Army Form C. 2118.

194 M.G. Coy Vol 10

Place	Date	Hour	Summary of Events and Information	Remarks and references to Appendices
Belgium	1/9/17		9591 A/Cpl HISLOP D. transferred from 70th Oh.G. Coy	F.O.
	2/9/17		The Company moved to STEENVOORDE' AREA	F.O.
France	3/9/17		The Company moved to LEDERZEELE AREA	F.O.
	4/9/17		Fine day. 104937 Pte McARTHUR J. evacuated 39th Gen Hospital	F.O.
	5/9/17		6645 Pte EELES. N.	
			90688 " GOSNEY. I. } joined	
			106524 " GOODWIN E.G. } From M.G. Base Depot	
			106644 " HAYES H.	
			102919 " HARRIS F.H.	
			73730 " HEALEY J.H. joined from A.H.T.D.	F.O.
	6/9/17		Wet day. 60342 Pte HOLDEN H.B. evacuated 14th F.C.D.	F.O.
	7/9/17		2/Lt C. E. HUGHES joined from the G. Base Depot.	F.O.
	8/9/17		57112 L/Cpl OSBOND C. declared a Deserter and struck off the strength	F.O.
	9/9/17		3 Officers and 50 O.R. proceeded to the line as a working party	F.O.

WAR DIARY or INTELLIGENCE SUMMARY

(Erase heading not required.)

Army Form C. 2118.

Place	Date	Hour	Summary of Events and Information	Remarks and references to Appendices
France	9/9/17		SS/130 Pte STONIER W Evacuated 4th Military Hospital	
	10/9/17		Very hot day	
	11/9/17			
	12/9/17		The Company moved to ZUYTPEENE	
	13/9/17		The Company moved to STEENVOORDE AREA	
	14/9/17		The Company moved to DICKEBUSCH AREA	
			Two sections moved into the line	
	15/9/17		Two gun teams also moved into the line	
	16/9/17		The remainder of the Company and transport moved to new camp	
			67321 Pte HARPER C. Wounded	
	17/9/17		SS/130 Pte STONIER W rejoined from hospital	
			Lt J.B. MOIR rejoined from course of instruction	
	18/9/17		16651 2/Lt DEWHURST.G. } Wounded and evacuated	
			89903 Pte BAULEY.A.E. }	
	19/9/17		The remaind of the Company proceeded to the line	
	20/9/17		The Company took part in the advance on the MENIN ROAD during barrage fire	

Army Form C. 2118.

WAR DIARY
or
INTELLIGENCE SUMMARY.
(Erase heading not required.)

Place	Date	Hour	Summary of Events and Information	Remarks and references to Appendices
Belgium	20/9/17		37052 L/Sgt WARREN W. ⎫ Wounded and	
			91157 Pte SMITH R.H. ⎬ Evacuated	
			34456 " DOWNIE G. ⎭	
			89223 " HOWES P.F.C.	
			S-7096 " HAWKINS W. Wounded at duty	
	21/9/17		SS-126 Cpl TUBB G. Killed	
			37437 Sgt RICHARDSON W.H. ⎫ Wounded and	
			84137 Pte EBLING J. ⎭ Evacuated	
			LIEUT N SMART Wounded at duty	
			The Company answered several S.O.S. calls and fired on Enemy	
			counter-attacks	
	22/9/17		Fine day. Dix gun and teams retired into the Fort and	
			enjoyed a shower	
	23/9/17		Fine day.	
	24/9/17		The guns and teams came out of the Fort in the morning and the	
			guns and teams was relieved at night	

Army Form C. 2118.

WAR DIARY
or
INTELLIGENCE SUMMARY.
(Erase heading not required.)

Instructions regarding War Diaries and Intelligence Summaries are contained in F. S. Regs., Part II. and the Staff Manual respectively. Title pages will be prepared in manuscript.

Place	Date	Hour	Summary of Events and Information	Remarks and references to Appendices
Belgium	25/4/17		The Company moved to the RENINGHELST AREA.	
			The enemy attacked in the early morning and the 4th gunner in the	
			front line, which had not been relieved, were lost.	
			6522 Pte GOUGH J.A. ⎫	
			27651 " PUGH T. ⎬ Missing.	
			55103 " COCHRANE F.C. ⎫ Wounded	
			104131 " EVERSON R. ⎬	
			LIEUT J.A. MATHESON Joined from M.J. Base Depot.	
			60342 Pte HOLDEN H.B. joined from evacuation.	
			The remainder of the gun teams from the front line came back	
			to the Company.	
			LIEUT B. MURRAY Transferred to ENGLAND sick 17.4.17 7.00	
	26/4/17		Fine day	9.00
	27/4/17		Fine day	9.00
	28/4/17		The Company moved to RIDGE WOOD AREA.	
			(One section went into the line on anti-aircraft duty	

WAR DIARY
or
INTELLIGENCE SUMMARY.
(Erase heading not required.)

Army Form C...

Place	Date	Hour	Summary of Events and Information	Remarks references to Appendices
Belgium	28/9/17		7615 Pte HAINS W. ⎫ Joined from M.G. Base	
			4364 " WATTS W.A. ⎬	
			42609 " WOODS J.A. ⎭	T.D.
	29/9/17		26224 " HARDY A. ⎫ Transferred to 20) ch.S.Cy	
			21500 " BLAYNEY T. ⎬	
			29992 " McKEON J. ⎭	T.D.
			27416 " PASTEAU L. ⎫ Wounded and evacuated	
	30/9/17		5786 " DONOHUE J. ⎬	T.D.
			25126 " SUMMERS A.J. ⎭	T.D.
			9591 Sgt HISLOP D. Transferred to 7th ch.S.Cy	T.D.

WAR DIARY
or
INTELLIGENCE SUMMARY
(Erase heading not required.)

Army Form C. 2118.

Vol 11

Place	Date	Hour	Summary of Events and Information	Remarks and references to Appendices
Belgium	1/10/17		The Company less one Section moved to BERTHEN AREA	
	2/10/17		One Section was relieved from the Line and joined the Company Hdq	
France	3/10/17		20160 Pte FORSYTH F.	
			44697 " MAXWELL J.	
			53338 " MILLER J. } Joined from the G. Base	
			24227 " HANDBURY G.	
	4/10/17		Fine day	
	5/10/17		3241 Pte KELLY H.	
			108169 " WOODBURN. W.	
			108322 " YARNOLD T.S.	
			43061 " MORRISON A.	
			84329 " GUNN A.F.	
			68227 " WHITE H.J. } Joined from the G. Base	
			66490 " SENTANCE E.	
			54255 " THEWLIS E.	
			106984 " TOWNSEND F.	

WAR DIARY
or
INTELLIGENCE SUMMARY.
(Erase heading not required.)

Army Form C. 2118.

Place	Date	Hour	Summary of Events and Information	Remarks and references to Appendices
France	5/9/17		60231 Pte WALKENSHAW A.	
			54260 " WATSON T. Joined from 6th S. base	
			10839 " DOWNEY J.	
			37804 " THOMPSON F.	
			2/Lt B.H. TYNDALL Furlined sick to ENGLAND 22.9.17	
	6/9/17		Very cold and wet day	
	7/10/17		36189 L/Sgt. WATERSON J.H. Joined from M.G. Base d.	
			Lieut BACHELAR E.M. rejoined from M.G. Base d.	
	8/10/17		55153 Pte BRASH F. evacuated sick	
			The Company moved to fresh billets in the same	
			area.	
	9/10/17		5786 Pte DONOGHUE J. rejoined from evacuation d.	
	10/10/17		Fine day	
	11/10/17		Company moved to WESTOUTRE	
	12/10/17		Wet day. 73803 A/g HARTLAND L. joined from M.G. Base	
	13/10/17		The Company moved to DICKEBUSCH	

WAR DIARY
or
INTELLIGENCE SUMMARY.
(Erase heading not required.)

Army Form C. 2118.

Place	Date	Hour	Summary of Events and Information	Remarks and references to Appendices
Belgium	14/6/17		Fine day	
	15/6/17		9432 L/Cpl MURRAY T Evacuated sick to N.C.C.D.	
			82344 L/Cpl REYNOLDS W.P. Evacuated from duty from Base	
	16/6/17		Two and a half sections went into the line	
			LIEUT N. SMART } Killed	
			55/136 Pte WYATT W.H.	
			43061 " MORRISON A.	
			55080 " CURRALL G. } Wounded	
			98060 " EDWARDS T.	
			67200 " BIRCHALL D. } Shell shock	
			55086 A/Cpl SHAW T.W. } Killed	
			58360 Pte BLAKEMORE W.	
	17/6/17		Fine day	
	18/6/17		Wet day	
	19/6/17		Fine day	
	20/6/17		1 Officer and 27 O.R. moved to WIZERNES AREA	

WAR DIARY
or
INTELLIGENCE SUMMARY.

(Erase heading not required.)

Army Form C. 2118.

Place	Date	Hour	Summary of Events and Information	Remarks and references to Appendices
Belgium	21/10		The transport less 5 vehicles moved to EECLE.	
			The Company who relieved from the line and moved to DICKEBUSCH AREA	
			60231 Pte WALKINSHAW.A. Wounded	
			103305 + HUMPHREYS A.H. Wounded at duty	
	22/10		The transport moved to WIZERNES AREA. The Company 5 vehicles entrained at VLAMERTINGHE and moved to WIZERNES AREA	
	23/10		The Company entrained at DICKEBUSCH and moved to same area	
			67200 Pte BIRCHALL D rejoined from evacuation	
			63355 Pte Jadon P evacuated Sick	
			55107 " Staunke C —	
			97625 " Serungaron J —	
			57111 " Jeunaut J a —	
	24/10/17		Fine day	
	25/10/17		Recitation of Awards by S.O.C. Sr Tranger HM joined from G Base.	

WAR DIARY or INTELLIGENCE SUMMARY

Army Form C. 2118.

Place	Date	Hour	Summary of Events and Information	Remarks and references to Appendices
France	26/10/17		Sergt Sherwood. G. evacuated Sick	
			316246 Pte Lyall. J.	
			116203 " Middlemiss E.	
			115811 " Hanagan E.	
			116339 " McGuickey P.	
			114440 " Cade W.	
			116239 " Hutton J.	
			117421 " Murray J.	
	27/10/17		311119 Sergt Robinson G reverted to pte	
			85097 Cpl Adams H. O	
	28/10/17		S.O.C. one day	
			128443 Pte Surrey J.	
			119375 " Ford J.	
			113974 " Gregory F.	
			117447 " Stewart W.	

Army Form C. 2118.

WAR DIARY
or
INTELLIGENCE SUMMARY.
(Erase heading not required.)

Instructions regarding War Diaries and Intelligence Summaries are contained in F. S. Regs., Part II. and the Staff Manual respectively. Title pages will be prepared in manuscript.

Place	Date	Hour	Summary of Events and Information	Remarks and references to Appendices
France	29/10/17		116987 Pte Rose B 116777 " Rayner S 14160 " Reynolds V } Joined from 1/9 Band	
—	30/10/17		Wet day	
—	31/10/17		Coy C's disinfection	

www.ingramcontent.com/pod-product-compliance
Lightning Source LLC
Chambersburg PA
CBHW081556160426
43191CB00011B/1944